TACTICS
OF LEGAL
REASONING

TACTICS OF LEGAL REASONING

Pierre Schlag and David Skover

Carolina Academic Press
Durham, North Carolina

L.C.C. Card No. 86-70367
ISBN: 0-89089-308-X, cloth
ISBN: 0-89089-309-8, paper

Carolina Academic Press
Post Office Box 8795
Forest Hills Station
Durham, North Carolina 27707
(919) 489-7486

CONTENTS

PREFACE

In teaching a variety of law school subjects, we have come to realize that many of the argumentative "moves" used by lawyers, judges, law professors, and law students can be attacked in fairly routine ways. These avenues of attack, these "tactics" or "counter-moves," follow fairly typical patterns.

We decided to identify and describe these tactics so that we could teach them directly to our students. This book is the result of our efforts.

Part I of the book is an outline that illustrates these legal reasoning tactics. Part II applies the tactics to attack the reasoning of four judicial opinions.

Obviously, we can make no claim that the outline is comprehensive. We have tried, however, to include the most persuasive counter-moves that are routinely used in attacking legal arguments. This means that both the simplest and the most sophisticated tactics have been excluded because they are unlikely to be used often.

As the introduction explains more fully, we divided the outline into three parts — premises, argumentation and conclusion — to mirror the rhetorical forms that legal advocacy generally takes, and we classified the avenues of attack within this three-part structure. Like all structures, ours may appear somewhat rigid or artificial. Indeed, there is a risk that the outline can be applied mechanically. But, ultimately, we believe that mechanistic thinking can be avoided only if the structures upon which it rests are exposed and explained. This is, in part, why we believe it worthwhile to provide our students and readers with the argumentative tactics typical of legal discourse.

Naturally, these tactics are rarely presented in the cold, pure form they are given in the outline. Rather, in practice, the counter-moves are embellished with detail and rhetorical flourish. That is an important point to keep in mind: the outline offers only logical possibilities for attacking a legal argument. It does not determine whether a particular attack should be used, nor when and how. These determinations depend upon the context in which the arguments occur, including the value commitments, the power relations, and the conventions of communication among the relevant participants.

We express our gratitude to Robert Bryan, Catherine Cruikshank, and Mark Giske for their generous research assistance and to Ronald Collins for his unfailing support in this endeavor.

INTRODUCTION

This book is designed to help lawyers and law students criticize and attack legal arguments. A legal argument can be seen as a series of "moves" designed to persuade the reader to accept a particular position. This book catalogues the "tactics" or "counter-moves" that are used routinely to attack legal arguments.

The book has two parts. Part I is an outline of the tactics most commonly used to attack legal arguments. Each tactic is identified and described in the outline. We have given a name to each tactic for ease of reference and of mastery. In addition, we have illustrated each tactic by applying it to attack arguments drawn from law, contemporary politics, and common knowledge. In every example, we first present the argumentative "move," and then we explain the suggested "counter-move." We hope that many of the argumentative moves seem familiar to you, because part of our aim is to show how even commonly accepted arguments are susceptible to attack by using the tactics.

Part II of this book contains a discussion of four judicial opinions often found in law school casebooks. The discussion shows how the various tactics described in the outline can be applied to attack the reasoning in these opinions. Although we discuss only judicial opinions in Part II, it is important to note that the tactics described in Part I can just as easily be used to attack arguments contained in legal briefs, legal memoranda, law review articles, and other pieces of legal advocacy. Moreover, the tactics can be used to attack all forms of legal argument, from technical doctrine to grand theory.

Indeed, the outline can be put to different uses. Some of the tactics contained in the outline will seem very familiar. If so, the outline can serve as a brief and convenient checklist of the possible avenues for attacking a legal argument, your own as well as those of others. Some of the tactics that we describe may well be unfamiliar. If they are, you will find that the outline is a useful source of new counter-moves to add to your argumentative repertoire.

How to Use the Book

As a first cut, perhaps the best approach is to scan the outline and get a feeling for its structure. We have divided legal argument into three parts: premises, argumentation and conclusion. When you examine an argument, the rhetorical form it takes often seems to track this three-part structure. First, there is the announcement of premises: those propositions that the reader is expected to accept at face value as true or correct. Then, there is the argumentation section, where the premises are combined and elaborated in a narrative designed to persuade. You can usually tell when argumentation begins because the text starts to link premises in various types of logical relations. Finally, there is the conclusion: the ultimate proposition which the argument is designed to establish.

With respect to each part of a legal argument, there are some classic types of objections to be made. It is because some tactics are often more relevant to premises, whereas others are often more germane to argumentation or to conclusions, that we have divided a legal argument into these three parts. However, just because the tactic is listed under one section of the outline (e.g., premises) does not mean that the tactic cannot be used to attack another section of a legal argument (e.g., argumentation). Moreover, be aware that a single problem in a legal argument often can be attacked by using several of the tactics described in the outline. For instance, a term such as "coercion" can be at the same time *imprecise, ambiguous,* and *incompletely defined.* [See pages 13–16] In addition, note that a problem that prompts objections in one part of a legal argument (e.g., the premises are *imprecise*) may well prompt objections in the other parts (e.g., the conclusion *lacks operational content*).

But, this is all getting ahead of the game. Before you can use the outline, you must be able to identify the various parts of a legal argument. This is not always easy. There is no mechanistic formula that guarantees success. The structure and meaning of a legal argument is a matter of interpretation. And, the author does not always make the structure of the argument obvious or clear. You will often have to reconstruct the argument that you wish to attack before you can determine which of the possible counter-moves will be the most devastating. Perhaps the easiest way to identify the structure of a legal argument is to start at the back end: what ultimate proposition is the author trying to get you to accept? This will be the conclusion. Once you have identified the conclusion, you can trace the argumentation back to the premises.

For instance, consider the following argument:

> The United States is committed to human rights and liberty. Leftist regimes, on the other hand, violate human rights and liberty. It follows that those who engage in armed resistance against Leftists are supporters of human rights and liberty. This follows because anyone who opposes Leftists must be opposed to the abuses of human rights and liberty that Leftists typically perpetrate. Accordingly, the United States should do whatever is in its power to help armed resistance to Leftist regimes.

Now, this is not a very good argument. If you were to use the outline to attack this argument, you would try to identify its various parts. Here you could say that the last sentence is the conclusion and the first two sentences are the premises; in between we have the argumentation.

Next, you could go to the corresponding part of the outline and check each of the propositions to see if it is objectionable. For instance, if you refer to the premises section of the outline, you will find a *lack of precision* in the first two sentences of the argument: what do the terms "human rights" and "liberty" mean? Lack of precision in premises does not necessarily defeat or impair the argument. Here, however, the lack of precision weakens the entire argument because, absent a specification of the meaning of these terms, there is no way of knowing whether opponents of Leftist regimes will be supporters of human rights and liberty or not. The same lack of precision is evident in the use of the term "Leftist." That term might well include any position from the liberal wing of the Republican Party to Marxists and anarchists. The lack of precision in the terms "individual rights" "liberty" and "Leftist" prevent us from taking the argument seriously. The imprecision of these terms carries all the way through to the conclusion that the United States should do all within its power to help armed resistance to Leftist regimes. Does that include support for armed resistance to the adminstrations of liberal Republican governors? It might well — according to this argument.

There are also problems in the section identified as argumentation. Look at the third sentence: "It follows that those who engage in armed resistance against Leftist regimes are supporters of human rights and liberty." This statement is objectionable because it is what we call an *improper movement in levels of abstraction*. The statement suggests that because persons are opposed to Leftists, they must therefore be opposed to every characteristic that Leftists have. More specifically, if some group is opposed to Leftists, then it must be opposed to the human rights violations that Leftists supposedly commit. But, that simply does not follow: people can be opposed to Leftists for lots of reasons that have nothing to do with human rights violations or liberty.

Look at the conclusion now. It reads: "the United States should do whatever is in its power to help armed resistance to Leftist regimes." We can already attack this conclusion on the grounds that the premises and argumentation are based on terms that lack precision and suffer from an improper movement in levels of abstraction. Is there anything else? The conclusion section of the outline suggests some possibilities. First, the conclusion *lacks normative content*. The conclusion is overinclusive: it is not true that the United States should do anything in its power to support armed resistance. Given the premises of the argument, the United States should only support armed resistance if that is consistent with and advances its commitment to human rights and liberty. There are other problems with the conclusion. It *lacks operational content*: it's not possible to determine where and when the United States should support armed resistance, since the key term "Leftist regime" is left so imprecise. Moreover, the conclusion adopts an *inappropriate frame of reference* inasmuch as it seems to mandate support for armed resistance to Leftist regimes regardless of whom this armed resistance might involve. This would have required the U.S. to support the Nazis during W.W. II, for instance. There are other objections one can make to this poorly framed argument; Part I will suggest possibilities.

Once you have read through the tactics in Part I, examine the judicial opinions contained in Part II. These four opinions, commonly found in law school casebooks, are analyzed in terms of the tactics of the outline. Application of the outline shows the weak spots in the reasoning — the gaps where the arguments are vulnerable.

When you use this book in attacking a legal argument, it will be helpful to think of the tactics as counter-moves in a game, rather than as descriptions of legal reasoning fallacies. Looking at the tactics as legal reasoning fallacies implies that there are objective errors out there existing in legal texts. If you go around thinking this way, there will be other people who will trip you up. They will do this by interpreting legal texts in ways different from yours. All of a sudden, those legal errors that you thought existed in the legal texts will seem to vanish. By contrast, if you look at the tactics as counter-moves, you will not be surprised when others answer your attacks with counter-moves of their own.

Indeed, the way you interpret or reconstruct an argument will affect which counter-moves are available for attack. Sometimes, you will have to deploy your attacks in the alternative. For instance, suppose that an argument reasonably might be interpreted to mean either X or Y. If so, then you will have to say something like this: "The argument means either X or Y. If it means X, then it fails because of *this*. On the other hand, if the argument means Y, then it fails because of *that*."

It is important to keep in mind that this book does no more than suggest possibilities for attacking legal arguments. What this book does not tell you is how you should actually present your attacks on legal arguments. Whether or not a tactic seems forceful when applied to a legal argument, or applies at all, is for you to decide. It depends upon the context, the values that are deemed relevant, the power relations, and a multitude of other variables which we cannot identify here. Simply because you attack a term for *lack of precision* or *ambiguity/ambivalence*, or you attack a legal distinction as a *false dichotomy* or an *overlapping opposition*, doesn't mean that your audience will agree. In fact, the audience might not even think that it matters. It's up to you to persuade your audience. What turns out to be persuasive will, of course, depend on what you are saying or writing to whom in what context where.

Part I
THE OUTLINE

1 / PREMISES

Premises are starting points in any argument. By definition, they are not argued for. Whether a premise is acceptable depends upon whether the author and the reader share a basis of common understanding that justifies the premise. In general, there are four commonly accepted bases that underlie the use of premises.

First, a premise may have an **empirical** basis. An empirical premise is either a statement of proven fact(s), or of generally known fact(s). An example of an empirical premise is: "the boiling point for water at sea level is 212 degrees Fahrenheit."

Second, a premise may have a basis in **authority**. An authority-based premise is accepted not because of its content, but because of the text or source from which it is drawn. Common legal examples include case precedent, the United States Constitution, lawyers' stipulations, tradition and custom.

Third, a premise may rely upon an **evaluative judgment** for its basis. The validity of such a premise rests on a political, moral, or aesthetic judgment or viewpoint that is shared by the author and reader. For example, the premise that "capital punishment is cruel and inhumane" is an evaluative judgment that depends upon a common moral or ethical viewpoint for its validity.

Fourth, a premise may be adopted as a **hypothesis**. That is, the premise is advanced conditionally to disprove its validity. This "reductio ad absurdum" proceeds by showing that acceptance of the proposition leads to absurd results or propositions. Suppose we assert the premise that "every right recognized by law is absolute." Then, if we show that each right must give way at times to another right when a conflict arises, we arrive at the absurd conclusion that "there are no rights recognized by law." This conclusion suggests that the hypothetical premise is wrong.

At times, it may be difficult to identify the type of basis that underlies a premise. A premise may appear to rest on more than one basis. Accordingly, in attacking a premise, it will sometimes be necessary to recognize the possible alternative bases for the premise and to attack each one.

The preceding discussion assumes that the premises of a legal argument are made explicit. Legal arguments may also rely on premises that are never expressed, called **implicit premises**. Identification of implicit premises is important to understanding the argument and to discovering appropriate avenues of attack. As a general rule, implicit premises may be identified by asking the following question: "Assuming that the argument is correct, what propositions in addition to the explicit premises must we necessarily assume for the stated conclusion to follow?" Of all the possible implicit premises in any argument, it is only worth questioning those implicit premises that may be controversial.

A. Attacks on Explicit Premises

1. Definition of Terms

a. Lack of Precision

Is the definition of a term sufficiently precise for the use that will be made of the term? If not, be aware of the possibility that we don't know when, where, or to what the conclusion reached applies. A term lacks precision if it does not set clear boundaries between what it includes and what it excludes.

Example 1:

"Most Americans support freedom of speech."

"Freedom of speech" is not a precise term. Does it include the right to circulate pornography, to incite riot, to extort?

Example 2:

"substantial"
"significant"
"reasonable"

These terms, as well as other imprecise "fudge" words, are commonly used in law. Note that they are sometimes intended to be imprecise.

b. Ambiguity/Ambivalence

If a term has more than one meaning, does the definition adequately identify the meaning intended? The problem of ambiguity or ambivalence does not lie with indefinite boundaries (i.e. lack of precision) but with the possibility of two or more meanings.

Example 1:

"The law must be designed so as to treat all persons equally."

Does "equally" here mean equal opportunities, equal outcomes, equal consideration or something else?

Example 2:

"We assume that a person can be punished only if the person intends to do a harmful act."

Does "intent" mean the desire to bring about the harm? Or simply the desire to do an act voluntarily, that incidentally results in harm?

c. Idiosyncratic Definition of Terms

If a term is particularly value-laden or politically charged, is the adopted definition uncontroversial? Or does the definition instead "borrow" on the moral or political charge of the generally accepted meaning of the term while committing us to a peculiar definition?

Example 1:

"Let us define our terms: infanticide is the non-consensual termination of fetal and other young human life."

Most people think that infanticide is wrong.Many people, however, might not think the same of abortion. By including fetal death within the concept of infanticide, the definition above forces us to talk about abortion as if it were a species of infanticide. The result is that the audience likely will bring all the negative feelings it has for infanticide to bear on the subject of abortion.

Example 2:

"What we mean by 'democracy' is nothing more or less than any system that holds and provides elections."

Given that most people are favorably disposed to democracy, this definition will lead them to favor political systems that hold elections. The problem, of course, is that there are political systems that hold elections and yet bear little resemblance to anything we would want to call legitimate government, much less democracy.

d. Incomplete Definitions

Does the definition rely upon a term that itself requires definition or further specification? Without further definition or specification, the proposed definition may be meaningless or indeterminate.

Example 1:

"Coercion is the threatened denial of rightful entitlements."

Unless we know what one is entitled to be, to do or to have, the definition is hopelessly open-ended.

Example 2:

"Privacy is defined as activity that concerns only one's self."

Unless the concept of "self" is well understood, this definition is seriously incomplete.

2. Empirical

a. Counterfactuals

Can the premise be refuted by known examples of fact?

Example 1:

"It is obvious that all cars are blue."

It is sufficient to defeat this premise to point to one car that is red. Obviously, this single counterexample will not defeat the proposition that "most cars are blue."

Example 2:

"You can't convict someone of murder for killing another human being without proving premeditation."

This premise can be defeated by showing that the crime of second degree murder does not require proof of premeditation.

b. Improbability

Is the premise improbable given other known facts and their implications?

Example 1:

"There are no pink Cadillacs in America."

Given what we know about the free market and American culture, it is doubtful that there are no pink cadillacs somewhere in America.

Example 2:

"It is assumed that no jury has ever consciously disregarded or rejected the instructions given by the judge."

This proposition is extremely unlikely given the great number of juries, the complexity of the law, and conceivable lay objections to the results that would flow from some jury instructions.

3. Authority

a. Correct Interpretation

Has the authority been correctly interpreted, and are there any other correct ways of interpreting the authority? There may be several conflicting, yet arguably correct interpretations.

> *Example 1:*
>
> *"The Bible states, 'An eye for an eye, a tooth for a tooth.'"*

Is this an authorization for personal revenge, a legal command defining the limits of just punishment, or a moral ideal?

> *Example 2:*
>
> *"Example 1 above applies only to eyes and teeth. It has nothing to say about anything else."*

Arguably, this is too narrow an interpretation of Example 1. Indeed, it seems reasonable to suppose that the maxim has a broader meaning. It might mean something like this: one harmful act deserves another.

b. Competence

Can the authority serve as authority for this premise? The problem here is that the authority may be an authority for some purposes, but not for the premise actually advanced.

Example 1:

"The Court will rely upon the testimony of an expert in engineering for the expert's views on psychology."

The expert's knowledge of engineering obviously does not qualify the expert to testify about psychology.

Example 2:

"Criminal law precedents on the insanity defense are binding for the availability of the insanity defense in tort negligence cases."

Nonsense. Given that criminal law and tort law serve different purposes by different means, it is arguably inappropriate to presume that criminal law can serve as authority for tort law, or vice-versa.

c. Competing Authority

Is there any authority that has been overlooked and that may undermine or contradict the authority relied upon?

Example 1:

"The common law clearly states that contributory negligence is a complete defense to the tort of negligence."

Yes, but what about statutes that have abolished contributory negligence in favor of comparative negligence?

Example 2:

"This statute allows prior censorship of newspaper articles criticizing public officials."

Federal and state constitutional guarantees of free speech and press no doubt will restrict the type of censorship that seems to be authorized by the statute.

4. Evaluative Judgment

a. Questionable Foundation

Is the political, moral or aesthetic theory supporting the evaluative judgment wrong, irrelevant, or inadequate generally for the legal system or for the particular legal issue at hand?

Example 1:

"We take as our starting point the view that the Constitution should be interpreted so as to maximize the *glory of the white race and the triumph of the American nation."*

Fascism is generally not an appealing political theory.

Example 2:

"The display of a woman's calf or thigh is manifestly obscene, and any movie that does so should be censored."

Nineteenth Century Victorian morals are probably not an appropriate framework from which to define obscenity in late Twentieth Century America.

b. Questionable Application

Even if the political, moral or aesthetic theory supporting the evaluative judgment is acceptable, the theory may have been misapplied or misconstrued. Are the factors that are taken into account in the evaluative judgment immaterial or improperly weighted?

Example 1:

"The deterrent effect of the criminal law on the insane will be significantly increased if the insanity defense is eliminated."

The legal theory that punishment serves to deter criminal behavior may have been misapplied here. If the acts of the legally insane are not voluntary, then they are not directly subject to deterrence.

Example 2:

"Self-defense should be proportional to the severity of the threat and the importance of the interest threatened. Accordingly, if an apple thief can only be apprehended by shooting him, one is justified in doing so."

Arguably, the elements of the self-defense standard have been improperly weighted in this example. The value of an apple is relatively small as compared to the response of shooting.

5. Hypothesis

a. Strawman

Does the argument correctly describe or characterize the view or proposition that the author wishes to defeat, or does the author instead mischaracterize the view or proposition, and thereby set up a mere "strawman" to knock down?

Example 1:

"Some people claim that there is excessive unemployment in the United States. We understand this claim to mean that there are no job openings available. The large number of 'help wanted' ads in American newspapers, however, indicates that there is no serious unemployment problem in America."

Arguably, this proposition mischaracterizes the nature of a claim that there is excessive unemployment in the United States. In all likelihood, the claim is not that there are no jobs available, but, rather, not a sufficient number. Accordingly, the argument above fails to defeat the true claim which remains standing after the "strawman" has been knocked down.

Example 2:

"The doctrine that the courts will not enforce unconscionable contracts is supposedly justified on the grounds that the courts are better able to construct agreements than the parties themselves. It is obvious, however, that the parties are better able to construct the agreements that they want. Accordingly, the doctrine of unconscionability does not make sense."

This proposition mischaracterizes the usual rationales that justify the unenforceability of unconscionable contracts: the absence of true consent, the lack of equal bargaining power, etc. Again, knocking down the strawman fails to defeat the real claim at issue.

6. Conflict between Bases

a. Covert Switch in Bases

Sometimes the basis for a premise is uncertain. This uncertainty allows the author to make it seem that a premise rests on a different basis than it actually does. For instance, the author may suggest that a premise rests on empirical grounds when, in fact, that premise is used to support an evaluative judgment. The problem with this "covert switch" is that the use which is made of the premise does not correspond to the reasons that we have been given to accept the premise. Although illegitimate, a covert switch is often an effective rhetorical device, insofar as it deflects appropriate avenues of attack.

Example 1:

"Major legal scholars seem to agree that courts applying the exclusionary rule release a number of known criminals."

Empirical? Authority? Evaluative? Be aware that this premise might be supported by one basis (e.g., authority), and yet, in the context of an argument, it could be passed off as resting on another basis (e.g., empirical).

Example 2:

"There is no connection in fact between lack of parental discipline and adolescent street crime."

This statement might carry the force of an empirical proposition, yet it may rest on nothing more than an evaluative judgment.

b. Inter-Bases Conflict

Even if a premise may appear valid on one basis, the premise may seem invalid in light of other bases. When this occurs, it can be difficult to choose which basis to prefer: should one choose the basis that validates or the basis that invalidates the premise? The inter-bases conflict occurs because one does not know which basis to rely upon in making the choice.

Example 1:

"In this case, we, the Court, must decide whether the Constitution guarantees a right to privacy. In interpreting the Constitution, we are bound to follow the intent of the framers and to render decisions that are morally sound. It is clear that the framers intended to leave privacy unprotected. By contrast, sound moral theory compels the conclusion that privacy should be protected. We have no doubt that established methods of judicial reasoning will enable us to resolve this issue, though at present we cannot perceive exactly how."

There is a conflict here between two premises that rest upon different bases (authority vs. evaluative). Because the conflicting premises rest upon different bases, it is not apparent which basis should serve as the ground to resolve the conflict. Must a decision to follow the framers' intent be justified on evaluative grounds? Conversely, must a decision to abide by sound moral theory be justified on the basis of authority?

Example 2:

"The Old Testament states that Moses parted the Red Sea by extending a rod over the waters. Of course, as an

empirical matter, the Red Sea cannot divide in half. If one is committed both to the authority of the Bible and to empirical considerations, how does one decide in what way to interpret the passage?''

Is empirical knowledge allowed to temper a literal reading of the Bible? Or is the Bible to be treated as a sacred text and interpreted free from empirical considerations? The inter-bases conflict arises because it is not clear whether the authority of the Bible or empirical considerations should be used to resolve these questions.

7. Problematic Ramifications

Even though a premise is acceptable in the context of the argument, nonetheless it may have undesirable consequences or implications for other settings.

Example 1:

"Race should never be a criterion in official governmental actions."

This premise may be acceptable when deciding whether the state should be allowed to discriminate against minority races. However, the Court's adoption of the premise in this context might well lead to its application in other contexts, such as whether governmental action designed to remedy past racial discrimination is valid or not. In this new context, the premise may well be undesirable because it would hinder attempts to remedy past discrimination.

Example 2:

"In defining constitutional protections of privacy, we, the Court, should refer solely to the common law to identify those human relationships that traditionally have received governmental recognition and protection."

This may be a satisfactory "inclusionary" premise, but not a satisfactory "exclusionary" one. In other words, this premise may be satisfactory in the sense that it extends privacy protection to important human relationships, such as the relationship of husband and wife. However, the premise may be unsatisfactory if it will be applied to deny protection of privacy to important human relationships that are not recognized by the common law, such as the relation of unmarried lovers.

8. Inquiry Preclusion

An explicit premise may be challenged here for two reasons:

a. Circularity

The argument requires as one of its essential premises the conclusion reached. Because the premise answers the legal question that is posed, all further argument is unnecessary to the conclusion.

Example 1:

"Our basic premise is that the Constitution gives the judiciary the power to interpret and apply the Constitution. We, the Court, know this because we have examined and interpreted the Constitution. And, from our interpretation, it is evident that we have the power to interpret and apply the Constitution."

This example is drawn from the celebrated case of *Marbury* v. *Madison*, 1 Cranch 137 (U.S. 1803). The obvious circularity is that, in order to establish the Court's power to interpret and apply the Constitution, the Court has first interpreted and applied the Constitution.

Example 2:

"The question in this contract case is whether we, the Court, should apply the law of Texas or New York to decide what rights are created by this contract. If we apply Texas law, then we would be expanding the rights of the parties under the contract. But we are forbidden to expand the rights of the parties. Therefore, we should not apply Texas law. New York law governs."

This argument is circular because it is not possible to say that Texas law would expand the rights of the parties unless one knows what law applies to the contract. Texas law would expand the rights of the parties by reference to what law? Certainly not Texas law. New York law? If so, then the Court has already decided to apply New York law. But that was the issue the Court was supposed to resolve: which law applies, New York or Texas?

b. Ideological Overstatement

The premise is an overstatement. It precludes examination of other evidence or argument bearing on the validity of the premise. Of course, all premises serve to shut down conflicting viewpoints. An ideological overstatement arises when the reader does not accept the scope of the premise, and rejects the shutdown of conflicting viewpoints.

Example 1:

"It is evident that contract law concerns only the interests of private parties."

This premise serves to exclude considerations of the public interest in the regulation of most economic arrangements.

Example 2:

"It is in the nature of legal rules that they be designed to maximize certainty and predictability."

Adoption of this premise would result in sacrificing considerations of fairness in the individual case, and of flexibility.

B. Attacks on Implicit Premises

1. General Attacks

One may make all the attacks listed above for explicit premises.

2. Process Objections

Reliance upon implicit premises automatically raises the possibility of a "process objection." The objection is that the author has not given adequate consideration to the validity of the implicit premise, and has thereby adopted an improper process for argument. Of course, this attack is only persuasive when the implicit premise appears to be both controversial and important to the argument.

2 / ARGUMENTATION

A. Attacks on Analogy

1. Unnecessary Parade of Horribles

A parade of horribles proceeds by demonstrating that a string of horrible or absurd results will follow if a certain position is adopted. The parade of horribles becomes unnecessary when it is clear that some very reasonable limitation on the legal position would eliminate the horribles.

Example 1:

"If abortion is legalized, this will lead to legalization of infanticide, euthanasia and, ultimately, genocide."

This argument is an unnecessary parade of horribles because termination of fetal life can be effectively distinguished from termination of post-natal human life.

Example 2:

"If the sale of handguns is prohibited, then it is only a matter of time before sales of rifles and shotguns are prohibited. In consequence, only criminals will have guns. Law-abiding citizens will be left defenseless and, ultimately, Western civilization will come to an end."

This argument parades a series of increasingly terrible horribles. The parade can be stopped at various points. The arguments for banning handgun sales do not necessarily require bans on the sales of rifles and shotguns. The former are easily concealable weapons, whereas the latter are not. Even if bans on the sales of handguns are extended to cover sales of rifles and shotguns, it does not follow that the citizenry will be defenseless: police protection will remain.

2. False Analogy

This rationale identifies X with Y. The fallacy, of course, is that X is not at all like Y in some crucial respect.

Example 1:

"Because society is like a biological organism, it must protect itself against poisonous foreign matter. Therefore, ideas based upon foreign ideologies should be suppressed."

There are many differences between society and a biological organism that make the analogy highly suspect. For instance, within a society, conscious political choices have to be made, whereas this is not the case with biological organisms. Moreover, arguably societies exist for the benefit of the individuals who are their member parts, but that is not true of biological organisms.

Example 2:

"Law is the mirror of society; it reflects the social and political values of its members."

Although law may "mirror" social and political values in some senses, in other, equally important senses, law may be used to generate, repress, or modify social and political values.

B. Attacks on Oppositions

1. False Dichotomy

A false dichotomy occurs where the argument treats two categories as exhaustive, when indeed there is a possibility of other categories that neither encompasses.

Example 1:

"It is clear that Marx did not believe that human nature is bad. One who does not believe that human nature is bad must believe that human nature is good. Therefore, Marx must have believed that human nature is good."

The problem here is the possibility of other options: that human nature is neither good nor bad; that human nature is not static, but rather malleable; that there is no such thing as human nature.

Example 2:

"A legal entitlement is either absolute, in which case it is a right, or it is not absolute, in which case it is a privilege. If it is a right, the state cannot take the legal entitlement away. By contrast, if it is a privilege, the state can deny the entitlement at will. In this case, the entitlement is not absolute. Therefore, it is a privilege and the state can deny it at will."

This argument presents a false dichotomy because a legal entitlement may fall somewhere in between an absolute right and a privilege. For example, a right may be conditional, or presumptive, etc.

2. Overlapping Oppositions

An overlapping opposition occurs when the argument fails to account for the fact that two positions which are defined as opposed or mutually exclusive in fact include elements in common.

Example 1:

"To decide whether some conduct is protected by the free speech guarantees of the First Amendment, we, the Court, must distinguish expression from action. Expression is

protected, but action is not. In this case, which concerns
. . . , it is clear that the defendant was engaged in action,
not expression."

Speech can clearly be both expression and action.
The distinction does not help when there is overlap.

Example 2:

"Liberty is the realm of activities that concern only oneself.
It follows that government infringes liberty when it
regulates 'self-regarding acts.' Therefore, government can
only regulate activities that impact upon others (i.e. 'other-
regarding acts')."

This argument sets up an opposition between "self-
regarding" and "other-regarding" activities.
Depending upon the perspective one takes, an
activity may be described as either "self-regarding"
or "other-regarding," or both.

3. Discontinuity

This occurs when the argument divides a conceptual
spectrum into two or more categories. The problem is
that there is no reason to set boundaries for the categories
at any particular points.

Example 1:

"Criminal law defines various types of mental states,
including specific intent, general intent, recklessness and
negligence."

These categories effectively subdivide a spectrum of state of mind, running from lucid self-consciousness to dimmed awareness of what one is doing. To the extent that the legal categories are used to differentiate punishment for crime, they may be criticized for dividing a spectrum in an arbitrary manner.

Example 2:

"A court can always apply the procedural rules of its own state. A rule is procedural, and not substantive, if it does not determine the outcome of a case. The rule at issue here would not determine the outcome of this case. Therefore, it is a procedural rule, and the state is free to apply its own rule."

This argument separates substance from procedure on this ground: whether a rule is or is not outcome-determinative. Over a large class of similar cases, certain rules are more or less likely to affect the outcome. But, it is frequently difficult to say that a given rule will always affect the outcome or will never affect the outcome. A classic example is the statute of limitations: is this a procedural rule or a substantive rule?

4. Misplaced Qualifiers

The use of a misplaced qualifier occurs when the content or scope of a concept, rule or standard is restricted by a limitation that does not fit, or that is not consistent with the concept, rule or standard.

Example 1:

"Rape is defined as sexual intercourse by a male with a female without her consent. There is no rape, however, if a man uses force to have sexual relations with his wife, even when she does not consent."

There is a misplaced qualifier here. The crime of rape requires that the woman not consent, except if she is the wife of the assailant. Why this exception? Isn't a wife a woman who might not consent to sexual intercourse with her husband? If so, shouldn't she be protected against such assault?

Example 2:

"Harm is a physical invasion that causes injury."

The qualifier "physical" is misplaced because injury can be inflicted, not just by physical invasion, but by mental disturbance as well.

C. Attack on Trading Off Meanings

During the course of the argument, the premise is redefined by being used in a different manner than originally posited.

Example 1:

(1) *Harms are defined by courts of law.*
(2) *Courts of law redress all harms as these are defined by courts of law.*
(3) *Therefore, all harms can be redressed in a court of law.*
(4) *Thus, no one can complain that justice has not been done on the grounds that his harm cannot be redressed in a court of law.*

Notice the possible switch in the meaning of the term "harm" from Proposition 2 to Proposition 3. Correctly read, Proposition 3 refers only to harms as these are defined by courts of law (i.e., "legal harms").

Example 2:

(1) *Taking a neutral position is the refusal to take sides.*
(2) *One can take the position of refusing to take sides.*
(3) *Of necessity, this position takes a side.*
(4) *Since it takes a side, it cannot be neutral.*
(5) *Therefore it is not possible to take a neutral position.*

Notice the possible switch in the meaning of the term "side" between Propositions (2) and (3). Arguably, Proposition (2) refers to "sides" that one refuses to take, whereas Proposition (3) refers to the refusal to take a side as a "side" itself.

D. Attacks on Levels of Abstraction

Some terms are more concrete or specific than others. For instance, the term "cypress" is more concrete than the term "tree," which, in turn, is more concrete than the term "vegetation." The preceding example demonstrates a movement from one set (e.g., of objects, of ideas, etc.) to larger, more comprehensive sets that include the original set. This is called a movement to a "higher level of abstraction." A movement in the other direction is a movement to a "lower level of abstraction."

1. Improper Level of Abstraction

The level of abstraction adopted in the argumentation is not appropriate to deal with the issue at hand. The problem is that, in terms of the issue posed, the argument is either too abstract or too concrete.

Example 1:

"The Great State of X needs to establish speed limits for ships, airplanes and cars. The standard should be based upon the average of the normal speeds of these vehicles combined."

If the problem is to develop speed rules for various types of vehicles, this approach adopts an inappropriately high level of abstraction. Arguably, the rules should differ for ships, cars, airplanes, etc.

Example 2:

"Having learned from Example 1 above, the Great State of X has a new vision: speed limits should be a function of the individual characteristics of the vehicles and the risks they pose. Accordingly, speed limits for sedans, sports cars and convertibles should be established respectively, as follows: 85 MPH, 60 MPH, and 40 MPH."

If the problem is to develop speed rules for cars, this approach adopts an inappropriately low level of abstraction. Arguably, basic speed rules for cars should not differentiate among types of cars.

2. Improper Movement in Levels of Abstraction

The inappropriate identification of a trait of a subset with a set, or vice-versa.

Example 1:

"A Rolls Royce is a transportation vehicle. A Rolls Royce has a grille. Therefore, all transportation vehicles have grilles."

This is an example of an inappropriate movement to a higher level of abstraction. Just because a Rolls Royce has a grille, it does not follow that all transportation vehicles have grilles.

Example 2:

"Homicide is a general category of crime that includes various gradations of killing. Murder 1 is a type of homicide. Therefore, Murder 1 is a general category of crime that includes various gradations of killing."

This is an example of an improper movement to a lower level of abstraction. Just because Murder 1 is part of a set that includes various gradations of killing does not mean that it also contains various gradations of killing.

3. Improper Combination of Levels of Abstraction

Legal arguments often call for reconciling disparate considerations, values, interests ("factors"). There are various ways of accomplishing this reconciliation, such as absolutism, priority ranking, balancing and reducing competing interests to a common denominator (such as dollars or utility). In using any of these techniques, one should choose a consistent level of abstraction for describing the various factors. If one does not, the argument may be open to the objection that it is "skewed." That is, by describing the factors at different levels of abstraction, the argument may have manipulated their relative importance or materiality, and improperly prejudiced the outcome of reconciling the factors.

Example 1:

"This First Amendment case requires the Court to balance free speech values against the state's interests in regulating

speech. Accordingly, the Court should determine the value of a particular speaker's speech, and see if it is offset by the general societal interest in regulating this type of speech."

In this balancing process, it may be improper to weigh the general societal interests against the interests of any one person. The problem here is that the levels of abstraction used to characterize the two opposed interests skew the results: arguably, one speaker's interests almost always will be subordinate to the interests of society at large. A more appropriate balance would be struck by comparing the societal interest in protecting speech versus the societal interest in regulating speech.

Example 2:

"This Court refuses to apply the unconscionability doctrine to bar enforcement of the parties' contract in this case. It is obvious that the defendant is seeking to avoid onerous obligations. While it is true that the defendant may not have been aware of the severe burden of these obligations at the time of contracting, nonetheless the security of transactions protected by contract law must prevail."

The Court's argument ranks society's interest in the security of transactions above the defendant's personal interest in avoiding unanticipated duties. Arguably, this priority ranking improperly combines values or interests characterized at different levels of abstraction. More specifically, the Court characterizes the interest on one side as the societal interest in security of transactions, and characterizes the interest on the other side as a merely private interest in avoiding unanticipated obligations. In performing the ranking, the Court should either have characterized both sides as representing societal interests or have characterized both sides as representing private interests.

3 / CONCLUSION

A. Attacks on Definition of Terms

The conclusion may be unacceptable for the same reasons identified in Section 1/A.1.

B. Attacks on Applicability/ Realization

One of the fundamental requirements of a legal conclusion is that it be capable of application or realization. That requirement may not be satisfied for any of the following reasons:

1. Lack of Power

Since application or realization of a legal conclusion by a court is likely to be affected by the scope of the court's own jurisdictional and remedial powers, and by the actions or beliefs of other actors [e.g., Congress, states, community], the court may lack adequate power to put the legal conclusion into effect.

Example 1:

> *"Lack of subject matter jurisdiction"*
> *"Failure of service of process"*
> *"Lack of case or controversy"*

These are examples of procedural and institutional limitations on the power of courts.

Example 2:

> *"Prosecutorial discretion"*
> *"Administrative misinterpretation of statutes"*

These are examples in which there is an absence of cooperation among necessary actors. Prosecutorial discretion or administrative misinterpretation may frustrate judicial or legislative attempts to bring about certain results. The courts and legislatures simply may lack effective mechanisms to compel exact compliance with their commands.

2. Lack of Operational Content

The legal conclusion cannot easily be applied because its terms do not refer to easily identifiable empirical entities.

Example 1:

"The Court concludes that contracts will not be enforced when they are the unfair product of unequal bargaining power between the parties."

We may have an idea of what "unfair" and "unequal bargaining power" mean, but it remains difficult to apply these criteria to distinguish enforceable from unenforceable contracts.

Example 2:

"The foregoing considerations suggest that a contract that is contrary to public policy will be declared null and void by the courts."

Even though it may be clear that nullity is the appropriate sanction for contracts that are contrary to public policy, it remains difficult to identify which specific contracts are "contrary to public policy," because the Court does not clarify the transactions that are "contrary to public policy."

3. Catch-22

The legal conclusion permits an actor to attain an objective only under conditions or within circumstances in which the objective cannot possibly be realized.

Example 1:

"Our conclusion is that social equality can only be achieved if the government acts in a 'color-blind' manner."

To the extent that our society discriminates on the basis of race, the standard of "color-blindness" may perpetuate social inequalities.

Example 2:

"We, the Court, conclude that we must look to the consequences of any proposed rule to decide a case. In this case, however, by looking to the consequences of any proposed rule, we find that this approach would itself bring about undesired consequences."

In looking to the consequences of proposed rules, the Court in this example becomes aware that deciding the case based upon the consequences will bring about undesired consequences. If this is true, the case should not be decided based upon the consequences. So, should the case be decided upon the consequences, or not?

C. Attacks on Justifiability

1. Lack of Normative Content

The legal conclusion can easily be applied to particular cases, but the applications do not correspond to justifications for the conclusion. The conclusion may be **underinclusive**, because the argument would require a broader or stronger conclusion, or **overinclusive**, because the argument would require a narrower or weaker conclusion.

Example 1:

"The narcotics admitted into evidence in this case were seized in a search incident to an arrest. All evidence seized in a search incident to arrest is admissible under the Fourth Amendment in a criminal trial. The sole purpose of this rule is to protect police officers' safety."

Arguably, this rule is **overinclusive**. If the only acceptable reason for allowing searches incident to arrest is protection of the police officers' safety, then narcotics seized in such an arrest should not be admissible, and the Court's conclusion is therefore too broad or too strong.

Example 2:

"In order to detect latent eye diseases, every person who needs new lenses or frames for glasses must obtain a prescription from a licensed physician."

If the only purpose of the rule is to detect latent eye diseases, then the rule is both **underinclusive** and **overinclusive**. The rule is **underinclusive** because latent eye diseases will not be discovered in individuals who do not need to wear glasses. The rule is **overinclusive** because the need to obtain new frames or lenses may occur more often than the need for a medical exam to detect latent eye diseases.

2. Frame of Reference Problems

A legal conclusion may be attacked from an empirical, authoritative or evaluative viewpoint or perspective not advanced by the author. In order to characterize aspects of reality, the author explicitly, or more often implicitly, assumes a viewpoint or perspective (a "frame of reference") that gives meaning to terms and categories. For example, the author may attempt to carve up and explain reality by using "models" properly called "sociological," "psychological," "moral," "economic," etc. When we make the claim that the author has advanced an improper frame of reference, we mean to suggest that this viewpoint or perspective can be faulted, for either or both of two reasons:

a. Inappropriate Frame of Reference

The frame of reference selected by the author misses an essential aspect of reality that is important for us to examine.

Example 1:

"The President of the United States concludes that his personal judgments based upon experience with Communists are a sufficient basis for deciding how to conduct foreign relations with Communist regimes."

If the President of the United States were to conduct foreign relations solely on the basis of personal views, this would appear to be an inappropriate frame of reference. Arguably, diplomacy based solely upon the President's personal convictions is unlikely to yield any effective and realistic foreign policy.

Example 2:

"A woman, who has been beaten severely by her husband for the past five years and who lives in constant fear of physical assault, kills her husband in his sleep. The Court concludes that the claim of self-defense is not available, because the woman faced no threat of physical harm immediately prior to the moment of the killing."

Arguably, the conclusion inappropriately narrows the relevant time frame for deciding whether a claim of self-defense should be available for this defendant.

b. Unjustified Frame of Reference

The author has offered no persuasive rationale to explain why the particular choice of a frame of reference is better than any other possible choice.

Example 1:

"The President of the United States announces that his personal experiences with Communists are a sufficient basis for deciding how to conduct foreign relations with Communist regimes."

If the President fails to offer any persuasive rationale for relying only on his own personal experiences, this would be an unjustified frame of reference.

Example 2:

"A woman, who has been beaten severely by her husband for the past five years and who lives in constant fear of

physical assault, kills her husband in his sleep. The Court concludes that the claim of self-defense is not available, because the woman faced no threat of physical harm immediately prior to the moment of the killing."

If the Court offers no reason for thinking that self-defense requires an imminent threat of harm immediately prior to the homicide, adoption of this time-based perspective would be an unjustified frame of reference.

Part II
CASE ILLUSTRATIONS

PROPERTY LAW

Pierson v. Post

3 Cai. Cas. 175 (N.Y. Sup. Ct. 1805)

This was an action of trespass on the case commenced in a justice's court, by the present defendant against the now plaintiff.

The declaration stated that Post, being in possession of certain dogs and hounds under his command, did, "upon a certain wild and uninhabited, unpossessed and waste land, called the beach, find and start one of those noxious beasts called a fox," and whilst there hunting, chasing and pursuing the same with his dogs and hounds, and when in view thereof, Pierson, well knowing the fox was so hunted and pursued, did, in the sight of Post, to prevent his catching the same, kill and carry it off. A verdict having been rendered for the plaintiff below, the defendant there sued out a *certiorari*, and now assigned for error, that the declaration and the matters therein contained were not sufficient in law to maintain an action.

. . .

TOMPKINS, J. delivered the opinion of the court. . . .

The question submitted by the counsel in this cause for our determination is, whether Lodowick Post, by the pursuit with his hounds in the manner alleged in his declaration, acquired such a right to, or property in, the fox as will sustain an action against Pierson for killing and taking him away?

The cause was argued with much ability by the counsel on both sides, and presents for our decision a novel and nice question. It is admitted that a fox is an animal *ferae naturae*, and that property in such animals is acquired by occupancy only. These admissions narrow the discussion to the simple question of what acts amount to occupancy, applied to acquiring right to wild animals.

————————— Discussion —————————

The Court frames a narrow issue to decide this case: what constitutes occupancy of wild animals? The issue can be framed in this narrow manner because the Court understands that occupancy is the method by which one obtains a property right in a wild animal. This understanding may be criticized as an *ideological overstatement*. Why should occupancy be the sole manner by which one obtains a property right in wild animals? As the dissent suggests, there are standards other than occupancy that could well serve to define the point at which one acquires a property right in a wild animal.

If we have recourse to the ancient writers upon general principles of law, the judgment below is obviously erroneous. Justinians Institutes, lib. 2, tit 1, s. 13, and Fleta, lib. 3, c.2, p. 175, adopt the principle, that pursuit alone vests no property or right in the huntsman; and that even pursuit, accompanied with wounding, is equally ineffectual for that purpose, unless the animal be actually taken. The same principle is recognised by Bracton, lib 2, c. 1, p. 8.

Discussion

The Court proceeds to decide the question of the ownership of the fox by reference to some very ancient authority. Citing Justinian (6th Century Roman law) and Fleta and Bracton (13th Century English law) the Nineteenth Century New York state judge announces that pursuit alone, or even pursuit accompanied by wounding, does not vest a property right in the pursuer. As the dissenter, Judge Livingston, points out, there is some question whether these learned authorities are truly *competent authority* on the issue posed in this case. The learned authorities had no knowledge of the rules and mores of the English sport of fox hunting in the context of Nineteenth Century New York culture. Presumably, the rules they devised were not designed to deal with this particular context.

. . . The foregoing authorities are decisive to show that mere pursuit gave Post no legal right to the fox, but that he became the property of Pierson, who intercepted and killed him.

It therefore only remains to inquire whether there are any contrary principles, or authorities, to be found in other books, which ought to induce a different decision. Most of the cases which have occurred in England, relating to property in wild animals, have either been discussed and decided upon the principles of their positive statute regulations, or have arisen between the huntsman and the owner of the land upon which beasts *ferae naturae* have been apprehended; the former claiming them by title of occupancy, and the latter *ratione soli*. Little satisfactory aid can, therefore, be derived from the English reporters.

. . . .

We are the more readily inclined to confine possession or occupancy of beasts *ferae naturae*, within the limits prescribed by the learned authors above cited, for the sake of certainty, and preserving peace and order in society. If the first seeing, starting, or pursuing such animals, without having so wounded, circumvented or ensnared them, so as to deprive them of their natural liberty, and subject them to the control of their pursuer, should afford the basis of actions against others for intercepting and killing them, it would prove a fertile source of quarrels and litigation.

However uncourteous or unkind the conduct of Pierson towards Post, in this instance, may have been, yet his act was productive of no injury or damage for which a legal remedy can be applied. We are of opinion the judgment below was erroneous, and ought to be reversed.

LIVINGSTON, J. [dissenting]

. . . .

This is a knotty point, and should have been submitted to the arbitration of sportsmen, without poring over Justinian, Fleta, Bracton, Puffendorf, Locke, Barbeyrac, or Blackstone, all of whom have been cited; they would have had no difficulty in coming to a prompt and correct conclusion. In a court thus constituted, the skin and carcass of poor reynard would have been properly disposed of, and a precedent set, interfering with no usage or custom which the experience of ages has sanctioned. . . . But the parties have referred the question to our judgment, and we must dispose of it as well as we can, from the partial lights we possess, leaving to a higher tribunal, the correction of any mistake which we may be so unfortunate as to make. By the pleadings it is admitted that a fox is a "wild and noxious beast." Both parties have regarded him, as the law of nations does a pirate, "*hostem humani generis*," and although "*de mortuis nil nisi bonum*," be a maxim of our profession, the memory of the deceased has not been spared. His depredations on farmers and on barn yards, have not been forgotten; and to put him to death wherever found, is allowed to be meritorious, and of public benefit. Hence it follows, that our decision should have in view the greatest possible encouragement to the destruction of an animal, so cunning and ruthless in his career. But who would keep a pack of hounds; or what gentleman, at the sound of the horn, and at peep of day, would mount his steed, and for hours together, *"sub jove frigido,"* or a vertical sun, pursue the windings of this wily quadruped, if, just as night came on, and his stratagems and strength were nearly exhausted, a saucy intruder, who had not shared in the honors or labors of the chase, were permitted to come in at the death, and bear away in triumph the object of pursuit? Whatever Justinian may have thought of the matter, it must be recollected that his code was compiled many hundred years ago, and it would be very hard indeed, at the distance of so many centuries, not to have a right to establish a rule for ourselves. In his day, we read of no order of men who made it a business, in the language of the declaration in this cause, "with hounds and dogs to find, start, pursue, hunt, and chase," these animals, and that, too, without any other motive than the preservation of Roman poultry; if this diversion had been then in fashion, the lawyers who composed his institutes, would have taken care not to pass it by, without suitable encouragement. If any thing, therefore, in the digests or pandects shall appear to militate against the defendant in error, who, on this occasion, was the fox hunter, we have only to say *tempora mutantur*; and if men themselves change with the times, why should not laws also undergo an alteration?

It may be expected, however, by the learned counsel, that more particular notice be taken of their authorities. I have examined them all, and feel great difficulty in determining, whether to acquire dominion over a thing, before in common, it be sufficient that we barely see it, or know where it is, or wish for it, or make a declaration of our will respecting it; or whether, in the case of wild beasts, setting a trap, or lying in wait, or starting, or pursuing, be enough; or if an actual wounding, or killing, or bodily tact and occupation be necessary. Writers on general law, who have favored us with their speculations on these points, differ on them all; but, great as is the diversity of sentiment among them, some conclusion must be adopted on the question immediately before us.

. . . .

Now, as we are without any municipal regulations of our own, . . . we are at liberty to adopt [the standard] that property in animals *ferae naturae* may be acquired without bodily touch or manucaption, provided the pursuer be within reach, or have a reasonable prospect (which certainly existed here) of taking, what he has thus discovered an intention of converting to his own use.

————————— Discussion —————————

In his dissent, Judge Livingston offers an altogether different standard to settle this dispute. He suggests that property in wild animals may be acquired without bodily touch, "provided the pursuer be within reach or have a reasonable prospect of taking." Arguably, the terms "within reach" and "reasonable prospect" *lack precision.* At precisely what point can we say that the pursuer is "within reach" or has "a reasonable prospect of taking?" It is evident that this lack of precision creates a *lack of operational content* in the conclusion. It is difficult to tell, under Judge Livingston's standard, at what point a property right arises in wild animals.

When we reflect also that the interest of our husbandmen, the most useful of men in any community, will be advanced by the destruction of a beast so pernicious and incorrigible, we cannot greatly err, in saying, that a pursuit like the present, through waste and unoccupied lands, and which must inevitably and speedily have terminated in corporal possession, or bodily seisin, confers such a right to the object of it, as to make any one a wrongdoer, who shall interfere and shoulder the spoil. The justice's judgment ought therefore, in my opinion, to be affirmed.

Judgment of reversal.

CRIMINAL LAW

State v. Hall

214 N.W.2d 205 (Iowa 1974)

UHLENHOPP, Justice

The principal legal question in this appeal from a conviction of first-degree murder relates to the effect upon criminal responsibility of a mental condition resulting from voluntary ingestion of a drug. . . .

The fact is not disputed that defendant slew Gilford Eugene Meacham in a car at the time and place charged.

. . . .

Regarding the incident involved here, defendant testified that casual acquaintances in California gave him a pill and told him it was a "little sunshine" and would make him feel "groovy." He met Meacham in Oregon and they made the arrangement for the trip east. Meacham had a pistol. Defendant drove all the way to Iowa without rest and was exhausted. He testified he took the pill at Des Moines, it made him feel funny, and the road turned different colors and pulsated. Meacham was sleeping on the passenger side. Defendant testified he heard strange noises from Meacham's throat, like growling. Meacham's face grew and his nose got long, and his head turned into a dog like the one defendant's stepfather had shot. Defendant testified he got scared, picked up Meacham's gun, and shot him three times. . . .

The County Attorney of Jasper County, Iowa, charged defendant with murder. A separate trial was held on the question of defendant's sanity to stand trial. A jury found him sane. Defendant pleaded insanity at the time of the act and stood trial on the murder charge; a jury found him guilty of first-degree murder. After the trial court overruled defendant's motion for new trial and sentenced him, he appealed.

In this court defendant [argues that] the trial court should have instructed the jury that defendant's drug intoxication, if proved, required an acquittal. . . .

I. *Drug Intoxication as Complete Defense.* The case is different from the usual one in which the accused contends only that use of alcohol or other drugs prevented him from forming specific intent. Here defendant first contends the drug caused temporary insanity, which constitutes a complete defense. Defendant is right that insanity, if established, is a complete defense. Under our law the test of insanity is "whether defendant had capacity to know the nature and quality of his acts and [the] distinction between right and wrong." . . . In addition to himself as a witness, defendant introduced testimony by two physicians who opined the drug was LSD and answered hypothetical questions about defendant's mental condition. By himself and those witnesses, defendant adduced substantial evidence which would meet the Harkness test in an ordinary case of an insanity defense. This evidence assumed the truth of defendant's testimony that he ingested the drug and sustained hallucinations as a result.

Defendant requested an instruction on insanity as a complete defense, tailored to include temporary insanity induced by drugs. The trial court refused it, and instructed that the jury should consider the claimed mental condition in connection with intent, as reducing the offense but not as exonerating it.

This court has held that a temporary mental condition caused by voluntary intoxication from alcohol does not constitute a complete defense. . . . Is the rule the same when the mental condition results from voluntary ingestion of other drugs? We think so. . . . Defendant does not contend that extended use of drugs caused him "settled or established" insanity. . . .

We hold that the trial court properly refused the requested instruction.

. . . .

MOORE, C. J., and REES, REYNOLDSON, HARRIS and McCORMICK, J J., concur.

LeGrand, Mason and Rawlings, J J., dissent.

LeGrand, Judge (dissenting).

. . . .

The insanity issue arose at trial because plantiff testified he had ingested a quantity of LSD shortly before the events in question without knowing what it was and without realizing its possible harmful effects. The majority concedes there was ample medical testimony produced by defendant as to the properties of this hallucinogenic drug to support a finding defendant was suffering from a mental illness or temporary insanity and to require its submission to the jury. However, the majority then deprives defendant of this defense by holding his condition resulted from the voluntary ingestion of drugs, which it equates with voluntary alcoholic intoxication.

. . . .

My first disagreement with the majority opinion deals with its premise that drug intoxication and alcohol intoxication are legally the same when considering them as a possible defense to the commission of a crime. . . . The fallacy in the majority's position is that it puts the issue on a *time* basis rather than an *effect* basis. It says the use of drugs is no defense unless mental illness resulting from long established use is shown because that's what we have said of alcoholic intoxication. . . . But we have said that about alcohol because ordinarily the use of alcohol produces no mental illness except by long continued excessive use. On the other hand that same result can be obtained overnight by the use of modern hallucinatory drugs like LSD.

. . . .

Our intoxication rationale as applied to alcohol simply does not fit the use of modern hallucinatory drugs; and it was never meant to. It was adopted before such drugs, as we now know them, were in common use. That is why I would say they *are* dissimilar and should be so regarded. There is no justifiable reason for equating the effects of so-called "hard" drugs, particularly those classified as hallucinatory, with the use of alcohol.

In the present case there is testimony of some 90 drug categories. Each has its own properties and each has its own effects. To treat all alike simply because each is classified generally as a drug strikes me as a judicial cop-out which completely disregards the realities of the situation.

In the case of alcohol, we have long experience which teaches us the usual and ordinary effects of alcohol upon the human mind and body. We are therefore justified in formulating general rules as to alcoholic intoxication, even though they may not operate with precise fairness in every case. We do not yet have the same scientific reliability on the effect of the use of drugs as far as criminal responsibility is concerned. But this should not tempt us to slough the matter off by lumping *all* drugs together with alcohol, where obviously many of them do not belong.

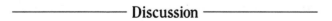

———————— **Discussion** ————————

The *Hall* court refuses to find that temporary

insanity caused by a one-time taking of an hallucinatory drug could be a complete defense to murder. The majority reaches its result by applying the rule that it previously developed for settled mental conditions caused by prolonged use of alcohol.

Judge LeGrand, in dissent, attacks the majority's reasoning as based on an *improper movement in levels of abstraction*. Apparently, he understands the majority to make the following argument:

(1) the complete defense of insanity due to alcoholic intoxication requires the defendant to prove a "settled or established" mental condition caused by prolonged alcoholic use;

(2) the complete defense of insanity for all drugs should be the same as that for alcoholic intoxication;

(3) here, the defendant did not prove a "settled or established" mental condition caused by prolonged use of hallucinatory drugs;

(4) therefore, the temporary insanity caused by a one-time taking of an hallucinatory drug did not afford a complete defense to murder.

This movement from a rule for alcoholic intoxication to a rule for intake of all drugs, including hallucinatory drugs, is improper in Judge LeGrand's view: it disregards differences between the mind-altering substances that are relevant in applying the insanity defense. Judge LeGrand identifies the "fallacy in the majority's argument" as failing to recognize that "ordinarily the use of alcohol produces no mental illness except by long continued excessive use. On the other hand that same result can be obtained overnight by the use of modern hallucinatory drugs like LSD."

Because the majority's reasoning is somewhat opaque, it is possible to interpret its argument as using no movement in levels of abstraction at all. Arguably, the majority only reasons that the one-time use of this hallucinatory drug is like the one-time use of alcohol. If so, the majority can be attacked for creating a *false analogy*. As Judge LeGrand counters, the majority's "time-based" analogy fails to recognize that an hallucinatory drug can, in a few hours, bring about the same disorientation that prolonged alcoholic abuse will induce.

CONSTITUTIONAL LAW

Lochner v. New York

198 U.S. 45 (1905)

MR. JUSTICE PECKHAM, . . . delivered the opinion of the court.

The indictment, it will be seen, charges that the plaintiff in error violated the one hundred and tenth section of article 8, chapter 415, of the Laws of 1897,[1] known as the labor law of the State of New York, in that he wrongfully and unlawfully required and permitted an employé working for him to work more than sixty hours in one week. . . . The mandate of the statute that "no employé shall be required or permitted to work," is the substantial

---

[1] *§ 110. Hours of labor in bakeries and confectionery establishments.* —No employé shall be required or permitted to work in a biscuit, bread or cake bakery or confectionery establishment more than sixty hours in any one week, or more than ten hours in any one day, unless for the purpose of making a shorter work day on the last day of the week; nor more hours in any one week than will make an average of ten hours per day for the number of days during such week in which such employé shall work."

equivalent of an enactment that "no employé shall contract or agree to work,"more than ten hours per day, and as there is no provision for special emergencies the statute is mandatory in all cases. It is not an act merely fixing the number of hours which shall constitute a legal day's work, but an absolute prohibition upon the employer, permitting, under any circumstances, more than ten hours work to be done in his establishment. The employé may desire to earn the extra money, which would arise from his working more than the prescribed time, but this statute forbids the employer from permitting the employé to earn it.

The statute necessarily interferes with the right of contract between the employer and employés, concerning the number of hours in which the latter may labor in the bakery of the employer. The general right to make a contract in relation to his business is part of the liberty of the individual protected by the Fourteenth Amendment of the Federal Constitution.... Under that provision no State can deprive any person of life, liberty or property without due process of law. The right to purchase or to sell labor is part of the liberty protected by this amendment, unless there are circumstances which exclude the right. There are, however, certain powers, existing in the sovereignty of each State in the Union, somewhat vaguely termed police powers, the exact description and limitation of which have not been attempted by the courts. Those powers, broadly stated and without, at present, any attempt at a more specific limitation, relate to the safety, health, morals, and general welfare of the public. Both property and liberty are held on such reasonable conditions as may be imposed by the governing power of the State in the exercise of those powers, and with such conditions the Fourteenth Amendment was not designed to interfere. . . .

The State, therefore, has power to prevent the individual from making certain kinds of contracts, and in regard to them the Federal Constitution offers no protection. If the contract be one which the State, in the legitimate exercise of its police power, has the right to prohibit, it is not prevented from prohibiting it by the Fourteenth Amendment. Contracts in violation of a statute, either of the Federal or state government, or a contract to let one's property for immoral purposes, or to do any other unlawful act, could obtain no protection from the Federal Constitution, as coming under the liberty of person or of free contract. Therefore, when the State, by its legislature, in the assumed exercise of its police powers, has passed an act which seriously limits the right to labor or the right of contract in regard to their means of livelihood between persons who are *sui juris* (both employer and employé), it becomes of great importance to determine which shall prevail—the right of the individual to labor for such time as he may choose, or the right of the State to prevent the individual from laboring or from entering into any contract to labor, beyond a certain time prescribed by the State.

This court has recognized the existence and upheld the exercise of the police powers of the States in many cases which might fairly be considered as border ones, and it has, in the course of its determination of questions regarding the asserted invalidity of such statutes, on the ground of their violation of the rights secured by the Federal Constitution, been guided by rules of a very liberal nature, the application of which has resulted, in numerous instances, in upholding the validity of state statutes thus assailed. Among the later cases where the state law has been upheld by this court is that of *Holden* v. *Hardy*, 169 U. S. 366. A provision in the act of the legislature of Utah was there under consideration, the act limiting the employment of workmen in all underground mines or workings, to eight hours per day, "except in cases of emergency, where life or property is in imminent danger." It also limited the hours of labor in smelting and other institutions for the reduction or refining of ores or metals to eight hours per day, except in like cases of emergency. The act was held to be a valid exercise of the police powers of the State. A review of many of the cases on the subject, decided by this and other courts, is given in the opinion. It was held that the kind of employment, mining, smelting, etc., and the character of the employés in such kinds of labor, were such as to make it reasonable and proper for the State to interfere to prevent the employés from being constrained by the rules laid down by the proprietors in regard to labor. . . .

It will be observed that, even with regard to that class of labor, the Utah statute provided for cases of emergency wherein the provisions of the statute would not apply. The statute now before this court has no emergency clause in it, and, if the statute is valid, there are no circumstances and no emergencies under which the slightest violation of the provisions of the act would be innocent. There is nothing in *Holden* v. *Hardy* which covers the case now before us.... *Knoxville Iron Co.* v. *Harbison*, 183 U. S. 13, is equally far from an authority for this legislation. The employés in that case were held to be at a disadvantage with the employer in matters of wages, they being miners and coal workers, and the act simply provided for the cashing of coal orders when presented by the miner to the employer.

. . . .

It must, of course, be conceded that there is a limit to the valid exercise of the police power by the State. There is no dispute concerning this general proposition. Otherwise the Fourteenth Amendment would have no efficacy and the legislatures of the States would have unbounded power, and it would be enough to say that any piece of legislation was enacted to conserve the morals, the health or the safety of the people; such legislation would be valid, no matter how absolutely without foundation the claim might be. The claim of the police power would be a mere pretext—become another and delusive name for the supreme sovereignty of the State to be exercised free from constitutional restraint. This is not contended for. In every case that comes before this court, therefore, where legislation of this character is concerned and where the protection of the Federal Constitution is sought, the question necessarily arises: Is this a fair, reasonable and appropriate exercise of the police power of the State, or is it an unreasonable, unnecessary and arbitrary interference with the right of the individual to his personal liberty or to enter into those contracts in relation to labor which may seem to him appropriate or necessary for the support of himself and his family? Of course the liberty of contract relating to labor includes both parties to it. The one has as much right to purchase as the other to sell labor.

This is not a question of substituting the judgment of the court for that of the legislature. If the act be within the power of the State it is valid, although the judgment of the court might be totally opposed to the enactment of such a law. But the question would still remain: Is it within the police power of the State? and that question must be answered by the court.

The question whether this act is valid as a labor law, pure and simple, may be dismissed in a few words. There is no reasonable ground for interfering with the liberty of person or the right of free contract, by determining the hours of labor, in the occupation of a baker. There is no contention that bakers as a class are not equal in intelligence and capacity to men in other trades or manual occupations, or that they are not able to assert their rights and care for themselves without the protecting arm of the State, interfering with their independence of judgment and of action. They are in no sense wards of the State. Viewed in the light of a purely labor law, with no reference whatever to the question of health, we think that a law like the one before us involves neither the safety, the morals nor the welfare of the public, and that the interest of the public is not in the slightest degree affected by such an act.

—————————— Discussion ——————————

In deciding the validity of a "labor law," the

Court seems to think that there are two classes of persons: those who are "wards of the state" and those who are capable of asserting their rights and caring for themselves [i.e., persons who are "sui juris"]. The Court uses this distinction to determine when it is constitutional for the state to regulate terms of employment. If persons are "wards of the state," it may be "in the public interest" to regulate their terms of employment; if, however, the persons are "sui juris," then the public interest is "not in the slightest degree affected," and a labor law regulating their terms of employment is invalid. Using this distinction, the court finds that bakers are not "wards of the state." Thus, a labor law regulating the working hours of bakers is not in the public interest and is invalid.

The presumption that a labor law is in the public interest if it protects people who are "wards of the state," but is not in the public interest if it protects people who are "sui juris," creates a *false dichotomy*. Simply because people are not "wards of the state" does not mean that they are not in need of state protection in employment relations, or that the public welfare would not be served by entitling them to such protection. Moreover, the very creation of the distinction between "sui juris" individuals and "wards of the state" may be a *discontinuity*. The capacity of individuals to protect themselves in employment relations runs a full spectrum, and it is unlikely that the differences in capacities would be organized neatly into the two categories of "sui juris" persons and "wards of the state." This discontinuity matters here, for the distinction "sui juris"/"wards of the state" establishes what is in effect an *ideological overstatement*: the court's premise is that if a class of persons (such as bakers) falls within the category of "sui juris" individuals, then that class of persons is not in any need of state protection.

Arguably, all of these objections may be refuted by reference to certain evaluative judgments drawn from "laissez faire" economic theory or Social Darwinism. Appeal to these theories might justify a distinction between people who are "sui juris" and people who are "wards of the state" for purposes of state labor regulations. Generally, opponents of governmental regulation of the economy found support in "laissez faire" economic theory and Social Darwinism for their beliefs that reasonable individuals, if left alone to pursue their own economic self-interests, would promote the public welfare as well. Moreover, it is possible that the Court relied on either or both of these two theories.

If so, it is possible to attack the Court's evaluative judgments as based on a *questionable foundation*. Arguably, these theories did not enjoy public acceptance at the time. Justice Holmes criticized the Court for deriving limitations upon state regulatory powers from "an economic theory which a large part of the country does not entertain." Furthermore, the theories might be considered morally repugnant or politically intolerable, because they denied any public interest in rectifying inequalities of economic bargaining power between employers and employees. In his dissenting opinion, Justice Harlan suggests that the New York legislators may have believed in the necessity of a labor law to protect bakery employees who "were not upon an equal footing" with their employers in bargaining for terms of employment.

Moreover, the Court's evaluative judgments may be attacked for *questionable application*. Assume that "laissez faire" economic theory is an acceptable foundation for the Court's limitation of state economic regulatory powers. Nevertheless, did the Court give serious consideration to the conditions of the labor market for bakery employees? Sufficient consideration to assert that the employees were able to "care for themselves without the protective arm of the State"? Did the Court provide adequate and convincing reasons for its assumption that bakers are not deserving of the same legislative concern as the miners and coal workers protected by the state laws upheld in *Holden v. Hardy* and *Knoxville Iron Co.*?

The law must be upheld, if at all, as a law pertaining to

the health of the individual engaged in the occupation of a baker. . . .

. . . .

We think that there can be no fair doubt that the trade of a baker, in and of itself, is not an unhealthy one to that degree which would authorize the legislature to interfere with the right to labor, and with the right of free contract on the part of the individual, either as employer or employé. In looking through statistics regarding all trades and occupations, it may be true that the trade of a baker does not appear to be as healthy as some other trades, and is also vastly more healthy than still others. To the common understanding the trade of a baker has never been regarded as an unhealthy one. . . .

——————— Discussion ———————

The court invalidates the New York act as a health law to protect bakery employees on the premise that the baker's trade is not an unhealthy one. The Court rests on "the common understanding" as *authority* for the premise. This premise can be attacked by use of *competing authority*. Indeed, Justice Harlan's dissent does so. His opinion relies upon contemporary medical treatises, statistical studies and congressional and state legislation to argue that there was no common or clear understanding as to the healthful conditions of the baker's trade. Moreover, Justice Harlan argues that the Court should view the New York statute as the best embodiment of the "common understanding" of the people of New York on the subject.

Furthermore, the Court refers to "statistics regarding all trades and occupations" to support its premise that the baker's trade is not an unhealthy one "to the degree which would authorize the legislature to interfere with the right to labor." If viewed as an *empirical* proposition about the frequency of injury and disease, the premise may be attacked by *counterfactuals*. Indeed, Justice Harlan's dissent cites to medical treatises establishing that bakery employees may be prone to particular ailments due to conditions uncharacteristic of other trades. Moreover, as Harlan suggests, the premise suffers from *improbability*. Presumably, there is a connection between excessive hours of labor and the worker's physical soundness and resistance to disease.

Quite possibly, the Court's premise that the baker's trade is not unhealthy was made to look like an empirical proposition by reference to statistics or an authoritative proposition by reference to "the common understanding," while it actually rests on an *evaluative judgment* of the Court. If so, the Court's reasoning would involve a *covert switch in bases*. In this way, the Court would lead us to believe as empirical or authoritative truth what is nothing more than the Court's evaluative hunch. This covert switch in bases arguably serves to deflect the criticism that the Court is substituting its beliefs for the New York legislature's policy judgment that more than ten hours of daily work in a bakery may endanger the health of the laborers.

Some occupations are more healthy than others, but we think there are none which might not come under the power of the legislature to supervise and control the hours of working therein, if the mere fact that the occupation is not absolutely and perfectly healthy is to confer that right upon the legislative department of the Government. It might be safely affirmed that almost all occupations more or less affect the health. There must be more than the mere fact of the possible existence of some small amount of unhealthiness to warrant legislative interference with liberty. It is unfortunately true that labor, even in any department, may possibly carry with it the seeds of unhealthiness. But are we all, on that account, at the mercy of legislative majorities? A printer, a tinsmith, a locksmith, a carpenter, a cabinet-maker, a dry goods clerk, a bank's, a lawyer's or a physician's clerk, or a clerk in almost any kind of business, would all come under the power of the legislature, on this assumption. No trade, no occupation, no mode of earning one's living, could escape this all-pervading power, and the acts of the legislature in limiting the hours of labor in all employments would be valid, although such limitation might seriously cripple the ability of the laborer to support himself and his family. . . . Upon the assumption of the validity of this act under review, it is not possible to say that an act, prohibiting lawyers' or bank clerks, or others, from contracting to labor for their employers more than eight hours a day, would be invalid. It might be said that it is unhealthy to work more than that number of hours in an apartment lighted by artificial light during the working hours of the day; that the occupation of the bank clerk, the lawyer's clerk, the real estate clerk, or the broker's clerk in such offices is therefore unhealthy, and the legislature in its paternal wisdom must, therefore, have the right to legislate on the subject of and to limit the hours for such labor, and if it exercises that power and its validity to be questioned, it is sufficient to say, it has reference to the public health; it has reference to the health of the employés condemned to labor day after day in buildings where the sun never shines; it is a health law, and therefore it is valid, and cannot be questioned by the courts.

. . . .

--------------- Discussion ---------------

The majority's argument at this point presents a classic example of an *unnecessary parade of horribles*. Give the state legislators an inch, and they will take a mile; there will simply be no way to stop them from regulating every aspect of all occupations and trades. The majority's argument can be attacked by showing that the New York act can be upheld as a health law on grounds that are adequate to distinguish the working conditions of bakers from those of other occupations. Justice Harlan offers just such grounds when he cites empirical evidence that the air quality and environmental conditions of bakeries were not as pure and healthful as those in other professions. Were the Court to sustain the New York law on these grounds, the parade of horribles would be arrested.

We mention these extreme cases because the contention is extreme. We do not believe in the soundness of the views which uphold this law. On the contrary, we think that such a law as this, although passed in the assumed exercise of the police power, and as relating to the public health, or the health of the employés named, is not within that power, and is invalid. The act is not, within any fair meaning of the term, a health law, but is an illegal interference with the rights of individuals, both employers and employés, to make contracts regarding labor upon such terms as they may think best, or which they may agree upon with the other parties to such contracts. Statutes of the nature of that under review, limiting the hours in which grown and intelligent men may labor to earn their living, are mere meddlesome interferences with the rights of the individual, and they are not saved from condemnation by the claim that they are passed in the exercise of the police power and upon the subject of the health of the individual whose rights are interfered with, unless there be some fair ground, reasonable in and of itself, to say that there is material danger to the public health or to the health of the employés, if the hours of labor are not curtailed. If this be not clearly the case the individuals, whose rights are thus made the subject of legislative interference, are under the protection of the Federal Constitution regarding their liberty of contract as well as of person; and the legislature of the State has no power to limit their right as proposed in this statute. . . .

───────────── Discussion ─────────────

The Court's argument that the New York regulation is not, "within any fair meaning of the term, a health law," rests upon its earlier premise that the baker's trade is not "an unhealthy one." The premise suffers from an *incomplete definition* of the term "health." At no point does the Court clarify the necessary and sufficient attributes of a "healthy trade." This incomplete definition is fatal to the argument, because the meaning of the term "healthy trade" is essential to the resolution of the issue. Due to the incomplete definition, the argument becomes totally *circular*: the New York law is not a "health law" because it regulates a trade that is not "unhealthy."

This interference on the part of the legislatures of the several States with the ordinary trades and occupations of the people seems to be on the increase. . . .

. . . .

It is impossible for us to shut our eyes to the fact that many of the laws of this character, while passed under what is claimed to be the police power for the purpose of protecting the public health or welfare, are, in reality, passed from other motives. We are justified in saying so when, from the character of the law and the subject upon which it legislates, it is apparent that the public health or welfare bears but the most remote relation to the law. The purpose of a statute must be determined from the natural and legal effect of the language employed; and whether it is or is not repugnant to the Constitution of the United States must be determined from the natural effect of such statutes when put into operation, and not from their proclaimed purpose. . . . The court looks beyond the mere letter of the law in such cases. . . .

It is manifest to us that the limitation of the hours of labor as provided for in this section of the statute under which the indictment was found, and the plaintiff in error convicted, has no such direct relation to and no such substantial effect upon the health of the employé, as to justify us in regarding the section as really a health law. It seems to us that the real object and purpose were simply to regulate the hours of labor between the master and his employés (all being men, *sui juris*), in private business, not dangerous in any degree to morals or in any real and substantial degree, to the health of the employés. Under such circumstances the freedom of master and employé to contract with each other in relation to their employment, and in defining the same, cannot be prohibited or interfered with, without violating the Federal Constitution.

The judgment of the Court of Appeals of New York as well as that of the Supreme Court and of the County Court of Oneida County must be reversed and the case remanded to the County Court for further proceedings not inconsistent with this opinion.

Reversed

———————— Discussion ————————

The Court's argument, in its entirety, may be attacked as *circular*. The Court begins with the premise that the Fourteenth Amendment protects the rights of individuals to purchase and sell labor upon the terms to which they might agree, unless a state imposes reasonable conditions on those rights by a legitimate exercise of the police power. Then, the Court establishes that an exercise of the police power is not legitimate if the state regulates the hours of labor of individuals who are legally competent to contract. Under such circumstances, the Court concludes, the state has interfered unconstitutionally with the rights of individuals to contract with each other in regard to their employment. Thus, the Court completes the circle: individual rights are defined in terms of the state's legitimate police powers; in turn, the legitimacy of police power exercises is defined in terms of the scope of individual rights.

Mr. Justice Harlan, with whom Mr. Justice White and Mr. Justice Day concurred, dissenting.

While this court has not attempted to mark the precise boundaries of what is called the police power of the

State, the existence of the power has been uniformly recognized, both by the Federal and state courts.

All the cases agree that this power extends at least to the protection of the lives, the health and the safety of the public against the injurious exercise by any citizen of his own rights.

. . . .

Speaking generally, the State in the exercise of its powers may not unduly interfere with the right of the citizen to enter into contracts that may be necessary and essential in the enjoyment of the inherent rights belonging to every one, among which rights is the right "to be free in the enjoyment of all his faculties; to be free to use them in all lawful ways; to live and work where he will; to earn his livelihood by any lawful calling; to pursue any livelihood or avocation." This was declared in *Allgeyer* v. *Louisiana*, 165 U. S. 578, 589. But in the same case it was conceded that the right to contract in relation to persons and property or to do business, within a State, may be "regulated and sometimes prohibited, when the contracts or business conflict with the policy of the State as contained in its statutes" (p. 591).

. . . .

I take it to be firmly established that what is called the liberty of contract may, within certain limits, be subjected to regulations designed and calculated to promote the general welfare or to guard the public health, the public morals or the public safety. "The liberty secured by the Constitution of the United States to every person within its jurisdiction does not import," this court has recently said, "an absolute right in each person to be, at all times and in all circumstances, wholly freed from restraint. There are manifold restraints to which every person is necessarily subject for the common good." *Jacobson* v. *Massachusetts,* 197 U.S. 11.

. . . .

It is plain that this statute was enacted in order to protect the physical well-being of those who work in bakery and confectionery establishments. It may be that the statute had its origin, in part, in the belief that employers and employés in such establishments were not upon an equal footing, and that the necessities of the latter often compelled them to submit to such exactions as unduly taxed their strength. Be this as it may, the statute must be taken as expressing the belief of the people of New York that, as a general rule, and in the case of the average man, labor in excess of sixty hours during a week in such establishments may endanger the health of those who thus labor. Whether or not this be wise legislation it is not the province of the court to inquire. Under our systems of government the courts are not concerned with the wisdom or policy of legislation. So that in determining the question of power to interfere with liberty of contract, the court may inquire whether the means devised by the State are germane to an end which may be lawfully accomplished and have a real or substantial relation to the protection of health, as involved in the daily work of the persons, male and female, engaged in bakery and confectionery establishments. But when this inquiry is entered upon I find it impossible, in view of common experience, to say that there is here no real or substantial relation between the means employed by the State and the end sought to be accomplished by its legislation. . . . Nor can I say that the statute has no appropriate or direct connection with that protection to health which each State owes to her citizens, . . . or that it is not promotive of the health of the employés in question, . . . or that the regulation prescribed by the State is utterly unreasonable and extravagant or wholly arbitrary. . . . Still less can I say that the statute is, beyond question, a plain, palpable invasion of rights secured by the fundamental law. . . . Therefore I submit that this court will transcend its functions if it assumes to annul the statute of New York. It must be remembered that this statute does not apply to all kinds of business. It applies only to work in bakery and confectionery establishments, in which, as all know, the air constantly breathed by workmen is not as pure and healthful as that to be found in some other establishments or out of doors.

Professor Hirt in his treatise on the "Diseases of the Workers" has said: "The labor of the bakers is among the hardest and most laborious imaginable, because it has to be performed under conditions injurious to the health of those engaged in it. It is hard, very hard work, not only because it requires a great deal of physical exertion in an overheated workshop and during unreasonably long hours, but more so because of the erratic demands of the public, compelling the baker to perform the greater part of his work at night, thus depriving him of an opportunity to enjoy the necessary rest and sleep, a fact which is highly injurious to his health." Another writer says: "The constant inhaling of flour dust causes inflammation of the lungs and of the bronchial tubes. The eyes also suffer through this dust, which is responsible for the many cases of running eyes among the bakers. The long hours of toil to which all bakers are subjected produce rheumatism, cramps and swollen legs. The intense heat in the workshops induces the workers to resort to cooling drinks, which together with their habit of exposing the greater part of their bodies to the change in the atmosphere, is another source of a number of diseases of various organs. Nearly all bakers are pale-faced and of more delicate health than the workers of other crafts, which is chiefly due to their hard work and their irregular and unnatural mode of living, whereby the power of resistance against disease is greatly diminished. The average age of a baker is below that of other workmen; they seldom live over their fiftieth year, most of them dying between the ages of forty and fifty. During periods of epidemic diseases the bakers are generally the first to succumb to the disease, and the number swept away during such periods far exceeds the number of other crafts in comparison to the men employed in the respective industries. When, in 1720, the plague visited the city of Marseilles, France, every baker in the city succumbed to the epidemic, which caused considerable excitement in the neighboring cities and resulted in measures for the sanitary protection of the bakers."

In the Eighteenth Annual report by the New York Bureau of Statistics of Labor it is stated that among the occupations involving exposure to conditions that interfere with nutrition is that of baker (p. 52). In that Report it is also stated that "from a social point of view, production will be increased by any change in industrial organization which diminishes the number of idlers, paupers and criminals. Shorter hours of work, by allowing higher standards of comfort and purer family life, promise to enhance the industrial efficiency of the wage-working class—improved health, longer life, more content and greater intelligence and inventiveness" (p. 82)

Statistics show that the average daily working time among workingmen in different countries is, in Australia, 8 hours; in Great Britain, 9; in the United States, 9¾; in Denmark, 9¾; in Norway, 10; Sweden, France, and Switzerland, 10½; Germany, 10¼; Belgium, Italy and Austria, 11; and in Russia, 12 hours.

We judicially know that the question of the number of hours during which a workman should continuously labor has been, for a long period, and is yet, a subject of serious consideration among civilized peoples, and by those having special knowledge of the laws of health. Suppose the statute prohibited labor in bakery and confectionery establishments in excess of eighteen hours each day. No one, I take it, could dispute the power of the State to enact such a statute. But the statute before us does not embrace extreme or exceptional cases. It may be said to occupy a middle ground in respect of the hours of labor. What is the true ground for the State to take between legitimate protection, by legislation, of the public health and liberty of contract is not a question easily solved, nor one in respect of which there is or can be absolute certainty. . . .

We also judicially know that the number of hours that should constitute a day's labor in particular occupations involving the physical strength and safety of workmen has been the subject of enactments by Congress and by nearly all of the States. Many, if not most, of those enactments fix eight hours as the proper basis of a day's labor.

I do not stop to consider whether any particular view of this economic question presents the sounder theory. What the precise facts are it may be difficult to say. It is enough for the determination of this case, and it is enough for this court to know, that the question is one about which there is room for debate and for an honest difference of opinion. There are many reasons of a weighty, substantial character, based upon the experience of mankind, in support of the theory that, all things considered, more than ten hours' steady work each day, from week to week, in a bakery or confectionery establishment, may endanger the health, and shorten the lives of the workmen, thereby diminishing their physical and mental capacity to serve the State, and to provide for those dependent upon them.

If such reasons exist that ought to be the end of this case, for the State is not amenable to the judiciary, in respect of its legislative enactments, unless such enactments are plainly, palpably, beyond all question, inconsistent with the Constitution of the United States. We are not to presume that the State of New York has acted in bad faith. Nor can we assume that its legislature acted without due deliberation, or that it did not determine this question upon the fullest attainable information, and for the common good. We cannot say that the State has acted without reason nor ought we to proceed upon the theory that its action is a mere sham. Our duty, I submit, is to sustain the statute as not being in conflict with the Federal Constitution, for the reason—and such is an all-sufficient reason—it is not shown to be plainly and palpably inconsistent with that instrument. Let the State alone in the management of its purely domestic affairs, so long as it does not appear beyond all question that it has violated the Federal Constitution. This view necessarily results from the principle that the health and safety of the people of a State are primarily for the State to guard and protect.

I take leave to say that the New York statute, in the particulars here involved, cannot be held to be in conflict with the Fourteenth Amendment . . . without bringing under the supervision of this court matters which have been supposed to belong exclusively to the legislative departments of the several States when exerting their conceded power to guard the health and safety of their citizens by such regulations as they in their wisdom deem best. Health laws of every description constitute, said Chief Justice Marshall, a part of that mass of legislation which "embraces everything within the territory of a State, not surrendered to the General Government; all which can be most advantageously exercised by the States themselves." *Gibbons* v. *Ogden*, 9 Wheat. 1, 203. A decision that the New York statute is void under the Fourteenth Amendment will, in my opinion, involve consequences of a far-reaching and mischievous character; for such a decision would seriously cripple the inherent

power of the States to care for the lives, health and well-being of their citizens. Those are matters which can be best controlled by the States. The preservation of the just powers of the States is quite as vital as the preservation of the powers of the General Government.
. . . The judgment in my opinion should be affirmed.

MR. JUSTICE HOLMES dissenting.

I regret sincerely that I am unable to agree with the judgment in this case, and that I think it my duty to express my dissent.

This case is decided upon an economic theory which a large part of the country does not entertain. If it were a question whether I agreed with that theory, I should desire to study it further and long before making up my mind. But I do not conceive that to be my duty, because I strongly believe that my agreement or disagreement has nothing to do with the right of a majority to embody their opinions in law. . . . The Fourteenth Amendment does not enact Mr. Herbert Spencer's Social Statics. . . . [A] constitution is not intended to embody a particular economic theory, whether of paternalism and the organic relation of the citizen to the State or of *laissez faire*. It is made for people of fundamentally differing views, and the accident of our finding certain opinions natural and familiar or novel and even shocking ought not to conclude our judgment upon the question whether statutes embodying them conflict with the Constitution of the United States.

. . . .

I think that the word liberty in the Fourteenth Amendment is perverted when it is held to prevent the natural outcome of a dominant opinion, unless it can be said that a rational and fair man necessarily would admit that the statute proposed would infringe fundamental principles as they have been understood by the traditions of our people and our law. It does not need research to show that no such sweeping condemnation can be passed upon the statute before us. A reasonable man might think it a proper measure on the score of health. Men whom I certainly could not pronounce unreasonable would uphold it as a first instalment of a general regulation of the hours of work. . . .

TORT LAW

Fletcher v. Rylands

1 L.R.-Ex. 265 (Ex. Ch. 1866)

[Plaintiff Fletcher was mining coal on property that he occupied as a tenant. Defendant Rylands owned land nearby. On that land, Rylands built a reservoir to run a mill.]

The judgment of the Court (Willes, Blackburn, Keating, Mellor, Montague Smith, and Lush, J. J.), was delivered by

BLACKBURN J. This was a special case stated by an arbitrator, under an order of nisi prius, in which the question for the Court is stated to be, whether the plaintiff is entitled to recover any, and, if any, what damages from the defendants, by reason of the matters thereinbefore stated.

In the Court of Exchequer, the Chief Baron and Martin, B., were of opinion that the plaintiff was not entitled to recover at all, Bramwell, B., being of a different opinion. The judgment in the Exchequer was consequently given for the defendants, in conformity with the opinion of the majority of the court. The only question argued before us was, whether this judgment was right, nothing being said about the measure of damages in case the plaintiff should be held entitled to recover. We have come to the conclusion that the opinion of Bramwell, B., was right, and that the answer to the question should be that the plaintiff was entitled to recover damages from the defendants, by reason of the matters stated in the case, and consequently, that the judgment below should be reversed, but we cannot at present say to what damages the plaintiff is entitled.

It appears from the statement in the case, that the plaintiff was damaged by his property being flooded by water, which, without any fault on his part, broke out of a reservoir constructed on the defendants' land by the defendants' orders, and maintained by the defendants.

It appears from the statement in the case . . . that the coal under the defendants' land had, at some remote period, been worked out; but this was unknown at the time when the defendants gave directions to erect the reservoir, and the water in the reservoir would not have escaped from the defendants' land, and no mischief would have been done to the plaintiff, but for this latent defect in the defendants' subsoil. And it further appears, . . . that the defendants selected competent engineers and contractors to make their reservoir, and themselves personally continued in total ignorance of what we have called the latent defect in the subsoil; but that these persons employed by them in the course of the work became aware of the existence of the ancient shafts filled up with soil, though they did not know or suspect that they were shafts communicating with old workings.

It is found that the defendants, personally, were free from all blame, but that in fact proper care and skill was not used by the persons employed by them, to provide for the sufficiency of the reservoir with reference to these shafts. The consequence was, that the reservoir when filled with water burst into the shafts, the water flowed down through them into the old workings, and thence into the plaintiff's mine, and there did the mischief.

The plaintiff, though free from all blame on his part, must bear the loss, unless he can establish that it was the consequence of some default for which the defendants are responsible. The question of law therefore arises, what is the obligation which the law casts on a person who, like the defendants, lawfully brings on his land something which, though harmless whilst it remains there, will naturally do mischief if it escape out of his land. It is agreed on all hands that he must take care to keep in that which he has brought on the land and keeps there, in order that it may not escape and damage his neighbours, but the question arises whether the duty which the law casts upon him, under such circumstances, is an absolute duty to keep it in at his peril, or is, as the majority of the Court of Exchequer have thought, merely a duty to take all reasonable and prudent precautions, in order to keep it in, but no more. If the first be the law, the person who has brought on his land and kept there something dangerous, and failed to keep it in, is responsible for all the natural consequences of its escape. If the second be the limit of his duty, he would not be answerable except on proof of negligence, and consequently would not be answerable for escape arising from any latent defect which ordinary prudence and skill could not detect.

Supposing the second to be the correct view of the law, a further question arises subsidiary to the fist, viz., whether the defendants are not so far identified with the contractors whom they employed, as to be responsible for the consequences of their want of care and skill in making the reservoir in fact insufficient with reference to the old shafts, of the existence of which they were aware, though they had not ascertained where the shafts went to.

We think that the true rule of law is, that the person who for his own purposes brings on his lands and collects and keeps there anything likely to do mischief if it escapes, must keep it in at his peril, and, if he does not do so, is primâ facie answerable for all the damage which is the natural consequence of its escape. He can excuse himself by shewing that the escape was owing to the plaintiff's default; or perhaps that the escape was the consequence of vis major, or the act of God; but as nothing of this sort exists here, it is unnecessary to inquire what excuse would be sufficient. The general rule, as above stated, seems on principle just. The person whose grass or corn is eaten down by the escaping cattle of his neighbour, or whose mine is flooded by the water from his neighbour's reservoir, or whose cellar is invaded by the filth of his neighbour's privy, or whose habitation is made unhealthy by the fumes and noisome vapours of his neighbour's alkali works, is damnified without any fault of his own; and it seems but reasonable and just that the neighbour, who has brought something on his own property which was not naturally there, harmless to others so long as it is confined to his own property, but which he knows to be mischievous if it gets on his neighbour's, should be obliged to make good the damage which ensues if he does not succeed in confining it to his own property. But for his act in bringing it there no mischief could have accrued, and it seems but just that he should at his peril keep it there so that no mischief may accrue, or answer for the natural and anticipated consequences. And upon authority, this we think is established to be the law whether the things so brought be beasts, or water, or filth, or stenches. . . . *Judgment for the plaintiff.*

—————————— Discussion ——————————

Lord Blackburn's rule describes when it is appropriate to hold a landowner liable for injuries to nearby land. The rule establishes that the liability of a landowner for injuries caused by things on his land should turn on two questions: (1) whether or not the thing was naturally there, and (2) whether the thing is likely to do mischief if it escapes. This rule can be attacked as based on an *inappropriate frame of reference.* It is certainly arguable that the two considerations are not the appropriate criteria for the imposition of liability on the defendant. The rule is biased in favor of low-risk uses of land as opposed to higher-risk uses; this bias may tend to favor rural, as opposed to industrial, uses of the land. The rule takes no account of the utility of the defendant's activity, nor of the level of risk prevailing in or acceptable to the community where the harm occurs.

Is Lord Blackburn's rule also based on an *unjustified frame of reference*? To answer that question, it is necessary to examine the reasoning that Lord Blackburn uses to justify his rule. He reasons that "[b]ut for his (the defendant's) act in bringing it (the thing) there, no mischief could have accrued, and it seems but just that he should at his peril keep it there so that no mischief may accrue, or answer for the natural and anticipated consequences." This *evaluative judgment* suggests that if the defendant's activity is a "but for" cause of the plaintiff's harm, this is a sufficient reason to hold the defendant responsible for the harm. To determine whether Lord Blackburn advances an unjustified frame of reference, we have to assess whether his evaluative judgment is acceptable.

Arguably, the evaluative judgment rests on a *questionable foundation*. The "but for" concept of causation should not be a sufficient rationale to hold the defendant liable. Just because the defendant's activity is a "but for" cause of plaintiff's injury does not mean that the defendant should be held liable. There are simply too many "but for" causes to an accident to rely solely upon the "but for" concept of causation to decide where liability for harm should be placed.

The questionable foundation of the argument becomes more apparent once it is recognized that Justice Blackburn's rationale has set up an *overlapping opposition*. It is not just the defendant's activity (reservoir) that is a "but for" cause of injury, but the plaintiff's activity (coal mining), as well as many other factors. One cannot say that either the defendant's activity is the "but for" cause of the injury or that the plaintiff's activity is the "but for" cause of the injury. Clearly, both are "but for" causes of the injury. Accordingly, the mere fact that an activity is a "but for" cause of some injury cannot be sufficient to allocate accident losses. There are too many "but for" causes to an accident to use the "but for" concept of causation as a sufficient rationale for allocating accident losses.

The case was appealed to the House of Lords. There, Lord Cairns reached the same result as Lord Blackburn, but announced a somewhat different rule.

> [I]f the Defendants, not stopping at the natural use of their close, had desired to use it for any puprose which I may term a non-natural use, for the purpose of introducing into the close that which in its natural condition was not in or upon it, . . . then it appears to me that that

which the Defendants were doing they were doing at their own peril.

Rylands v. *Fletcher*, 3 L.R.-H.L. 330, 339 (1868)

This rule adds a new requirement for liability: the harm must stem from a "non-natural use" of the land. The new limitation avoids some of the problems which made Lord Blackburn's rule appear to be an inappropriate frame of reference. Now the rule seems to take into account the prevailing level of risk in the community and the appropriateness of the use made of the land. But, while the rule now seems to avoid an inappropriate frame of reference, the rule *lacks operational content*. What is or is not a natural use of the land? Does the answer depend upon the land uses prevailing in the community? Which community? Do we take the utility of the use into account? If so, how much?

One modern version of the strict liability rule announced by Lord Cairns is to be found in the definition of ultrahazardous activities. Section 520 of the Second Restatement of Torts, for instance, states:

In determining whether an activity is abnormally dangerous, the following factors are to be considered:

(a) existence of a high degree of risk of some harm to the person, land or chattels of others;

(b) likelihood that the harm that results from it will be great;

(c) inability to eliminate the risk by the exercise of reasonable care;

(d) extent to which the activity is not a matter of common usage;

(e) inappropriateness of the activity to the place where it is carried on; and

(f) extent to which its value to the community is out-weighed by its dangerous attributes."

RESTATEMENT (SECOND) OF TORTS §520
(1977)

This definition of ultrahazardous activities arguably suffers even more greatly from a *lack of operational content* than Lord Cairns' rule. Under this test, it is extremely difficult to determine what human activity will be deemed ultrahazardous, when, or where. Multifactor tests, such as this one, are often objectionable because they lack operational content.

About the Authors

Pierre Schlag and David Skover are Associate Professors at the University of Puget Sound School of Law. Professor Schlag received his B.A. from Yale University and his J.D. from UCLA School of Law. After graduation, he was a research fellow at the Institute of European Studies in Brussels, Belgium and then went on to practice with the Washington, D.C. law firm of Covington & Burling. Professor Skover received his B.A. from Princeton University and his J.D. from Yale University Law School. He then clerked for Judge Jon O. Newman of the U.S. Court of Appeals for the Second Circuit.